Table of Contents

Pearl Harbor   3
Photo Glossary   15
Index   16
About the Author   16

Can you find these words?

forces

memorials

mourn

sacrifice

Pearl Harbor

A symbol stands for an idea.

Pearl Harbor is a military base.

It is a symbol of **sacrifice.**

Pearl Harbor is near Honolulu, Hawaii. It was attacked in 1941.

Japanese **forces** sunk ships. They destroyed airplanes.

Thousands of people died.
The United States went to war.

There are many **memorials** at Pearl Harbor.

People visit Pearl Harbor to remember.

They visit to **mourn** the lost lives.

Did you find these words?

Japanese **forces** sunk ships.

There are many **memorials** at Pearl Harbor.

They visit to **mourn** the lost lives.

It is a symbol of **sacrifice**.

Photo Glossary

 **forces** (FORS-ez): Organizations authorized by countries to use weapons and deadly force to support their countries' interests.

 **memorials** (muh-MOR-ee-uhls): Things built, such as statues or monuments, to help people remember events or people.

 **mourn** (morn): To feel and show that you are sad for a death or a loss.

 **sacrifice** (SAK-ruh-fise): To give up something for the sake of something that is more important.

Index

base 4
Hawaii 6
Honolulu 6
Japanese 8
ships 8
United States 9

About the Author

K.A. Robertson is a writer and editor who enjoys learning about the history of the United States. She is grateful to those who fight for freedom and equality for all people.

© 2020 Rourke Educational Media

All rights reserved. No part of this book may be reproduced or utilized in any form or by any means, electronic or mechanical including photocopying, recording, or by any information storage and retrieval system without permission in writing from the publisher.

www.rourkeeducationalmedia.com

PHOTO CREDITS: Cover: ©pinggr; Pg 2, 10, 14, 15 ©jewhyte; Pg 2, 12, 14, 15, ©HaizhanZheng; Pg 2, 4, 14, 15, ©gregobagel; Pg 2, 8, 14, 15 ©Everett Historical; Pg 3 ©asiseeit; Pg 6 ©jewhyte

Edited by: Kim Thompson
Cover and interior design by: Kathy Walsh

Library of Congress PCN Data
Pearl Harbor / K.A. Robertson
(Visiting U.S. Symbols)
ISBN 978-1-73160-573-3 (hard cover)(alk. paper)
ISBN 978-1-73160-421-7 (soft cover)
ISBN 978-1-73160-622-8 (e-Book)
ISBN 978-1-73160-658-7 (ePub)
Library of Congress Control Number: 2018967350

Printed in the United States of America,
North Mankato, Minnesota